Discoverin

FOR THE TWO MILLION PEOPLE who visit Bat
Or does it? Visitors from around the world flock
the ancient Roman Baths, the extra-ordinary range shops, and the restaurants.

But to me, Bath is much more. Bath *is* 2,000 years of history. A history as extra-ordinary as the hot spa water which bubbles from the ground at a constant rate of over a million litres a day. A history so rich that every nook and cranny of this wonderful City reveals a fascinating new twist to a string of rich, famous and Royal people.

My love of Bath and its gorgeous history has borne fruit in this guide, unique in that all is by hand. Nearly 100 detailed illustrations, each with a hand written commentary, are linked together into a walking tour of Bath. Each double page spread, however, focusses on just one of the City's famous aspects, be it the Abbey, the Canal, the Baths, Pierrepont St. et.c..

I hope you enjoy my book; I hope it is as pleasant to browse through in an evening as it is useful in exploring the City. As educational as it is artistic. As fun as it is serious.

Discovering Bath.......... come exploring with us.......

The Snowdon family *(Paul, Sue and three children - Matthew, Claire and James)* live close to Bath; I *(Paul)* am utterly addicted to drawing - as this book shows!

Page	Contents

THE WALK

1 THE WALK STARTS in Royal Victoria Park, or at any point along the route *(see map on pages 20-21)*

FEEDING THE DUCKS in Royal Victoria Park. Opened by Princess Victoria in 1830 *(before she became Queen)*, the park's 53 acres of grass and gardens are a credit to the city.

ONE WAY LOVE – As you leave the Park pass the magnificent obelisk *(pictured)* erected to celebrate Queen Victoria's coming of age. Alas, the City's gesture was not reciprocated. The princess was just 11 years old when she opened the park and had become bored. She vowed never to return to Bath again – a vow that she kept.

Perhaps her visit inspired the three stone lions around the monument, all sporting different expressions; one is bored and sleepy, another resolute, and the third quizzical. The medallions on the three sides of the triangular monument chronicle Queen Victorias life, romance and death.

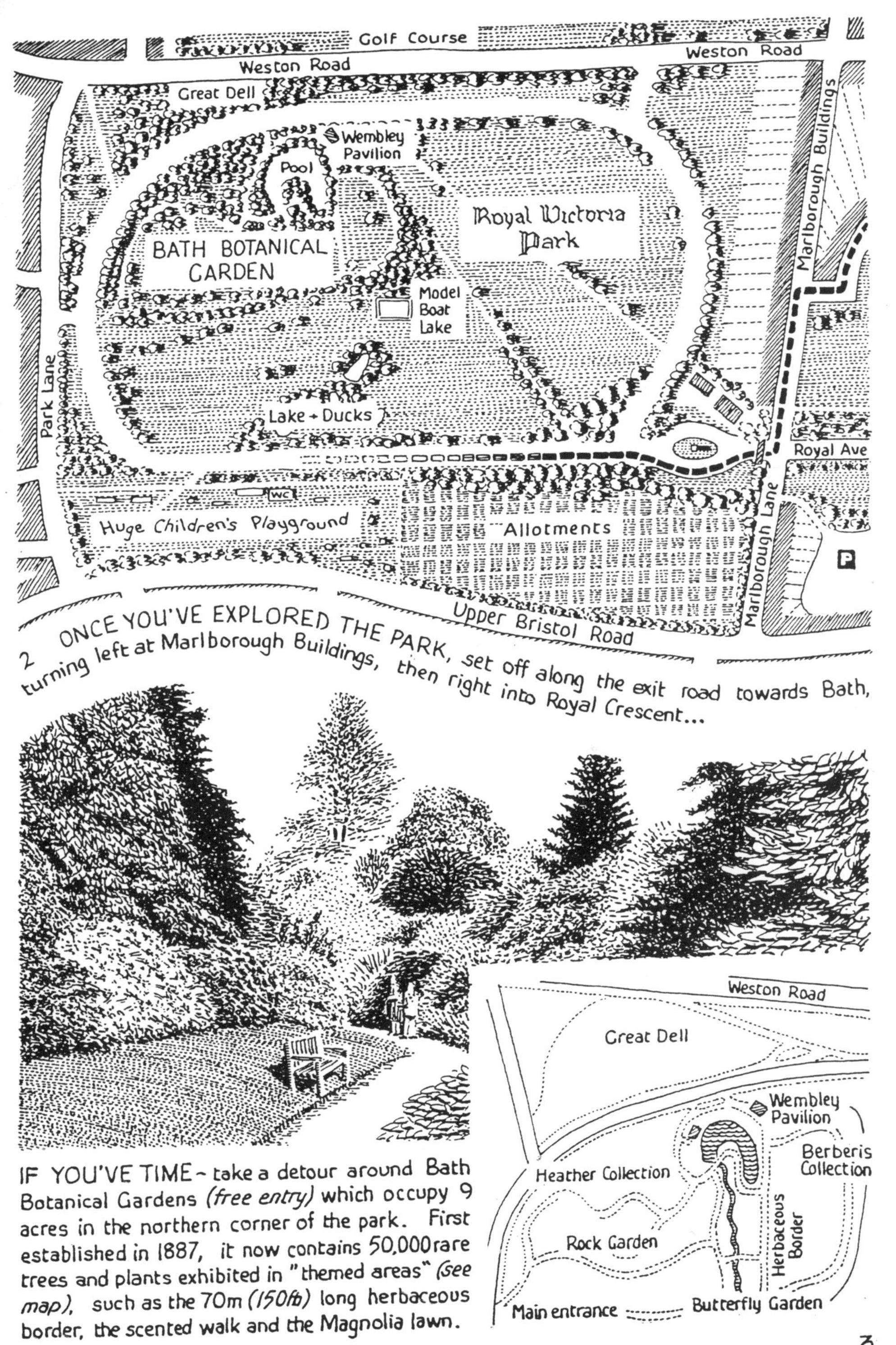

2 ONCE YOU'VE EXPLORED THE PARK, set off along the exit road towards Bath, turning left at Marlborough Buildings, then right into Royal Crescent...

IF YOU'VE TIME – take a detour around Bath Botanical Gardens *(free entry)* which occupy 9 acres in the northern corner of the park. First established in 1887, it now contains 50,000 rare trees and plants exhibited in "themed areas" *(see map)*, such as the 70m *(150ft)* long herbaceous border, the scented walk and the Magnolia lawn.

GEORGIAN CURVES

Royal Crescent and The Circus

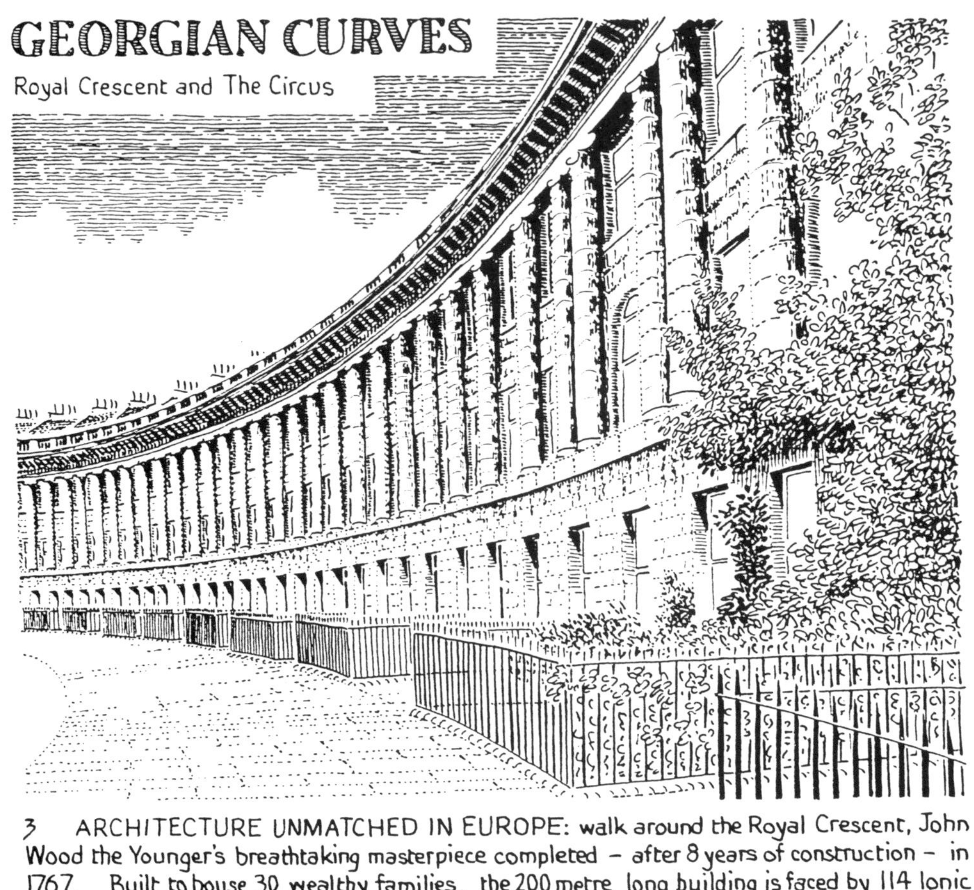

3 ARCHITECTURE UNMATCHED IN EUROPE: walk around the Royal Crescent, John Wood the Younger's breathtaking masterpiece completed – after 8 years of construction – in 1767. Built to house 30 wealthy families, the 200 metre long building is faced by 114 Ionic columns, regularly spaced around the Crescent apart from two double pillars which mark – almost invisibly – its centre *(see picture above)*. The whole effect when viewed from the park below *(see picture on page 40)* is stunning: surely this must be Europe's greatest single architectural entity? "Number 1 Royal Crescent" – the first house to be built – was originally the home of the Duke of York and has been lovingly restored to its original Georgian style by the Bath Preservation Trust; it is now open to the Public as a museum. Further around the Crescent Isaac Pitman, famous to secretaries around the world as the inventor of shorthand writing, lived at number 12, whilst number 15 looks almost anonymous until you reach the front door and realise it houses the sumptuous, 45 bedroom "[illegible] Hotel, – which was recently sold for £8 million [illegible] ing.

4 BROCK STREET: to John Woo[illegible] this walk is the wrong way round! He w[illegible] prefer that admirers approach his Roy[illegible] Crescent from Brock Street, which he [illegible] designed in modest style to make the Cre[illegible] more grand by contrast. Thomas Brock [illegible] John Wood's father in law.

KNOW YOUR COLUMNS:

How to recognise the three classical orders:

Doric

Ionic

Corinthian

Margaret's Buildings, on the left, is a lovely [illegible] of antique, health food and book shops.

5 JOHN WOOD THE ELDER started "The Circus" *(picture left)* in 1754 - the year he died. Inspired by his life long ambition to build a 'new Rome' in Bath, John designed the Circus as an 'inside-out Colosseum' with 3 layers of frieze supported by Doric, Ionic and Corinthian Columns. As if to add to its mystical qualities, the Circus is the same diameter as Stonehenge. The massive plane trees in its centre were a later addition; when first built the 'arena' was cobbled with a central reservoir.

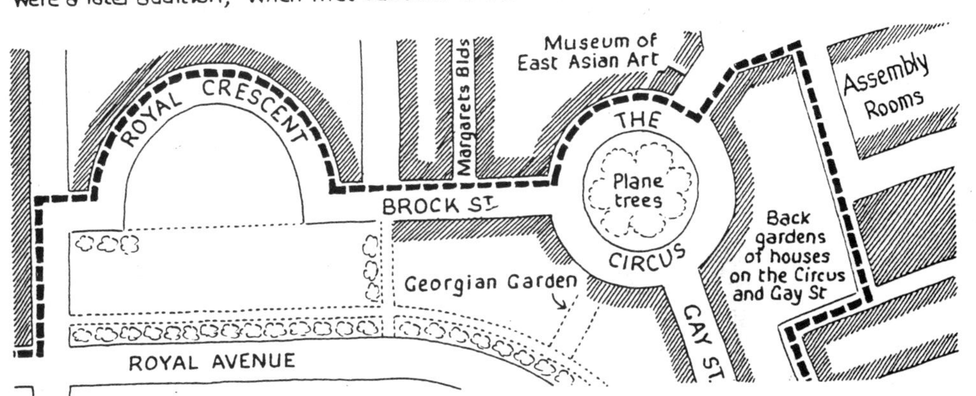

CELEBRITY CIRCUS: many a famous character in history has lived in the Circus - including William Pitt *Prime Minister* (No.7-8) and Thom^s Gainsborough *Artist* at No. 17. Also ....

DAVID LIVINGSTONE *African explorer* 1813-73 lived at number 13

W E GLADSTONE - *statesman* lived at number 27 when not at the House of Commons.

LORD CLIVE OF INDIA (1725-74) lived at Number 11 The Circus.

6 "ONE OF THE FINEST SUITES OF ROOMS IN EUROPE" - leave The Circus by Bennett St to find the Assembly Rooms *(pictured)*. Designed by John Wood the Younger and opened in 1771, this was the focus of Bath's elegant social life for 150 years; led by Richard "Beau" Nash *(above)* and immortalised in the writings of Sheridan, Dickens and Jane Austen. Recently restored by the National Trust from World War II bomb damage, the basement houses a costume museum.

SHOPPING IN BATH

7 HEAD SOUTH from the Assembly Rooms and *meander* through Bath's famous shopping centre *(see maps on pages 14-15 and 20-21)*. Delightful alleyways crammed with quaint little shops *(pictured lower right)* intermingle with grandiose Georgian streets like Milsom Street *(upper right)* and Union St. *(below)* whose large stores stand tall and proud, facing each other as if in a guard of honour. Eventually, head towards Pulteney Bridge......

8 SHOPPERS CROWD INTO UNION STREET heading south towards Stall Street.

JOLLYS on Milsom St, est. 165 years ago, is one of Baths most prestigious department stores.

JANE AUSTEN wrote in her book *Northanger Abbey* "Bath is such a charming place, sir, there are so many good shops here". 200 years later the words are still true; Bath claims to be Britains premiere shopping centre outside London with a bewildering variety of over 700 shops.

NORTHUMBERLAND PLACE is one of Bath's many delightful alleyways crammed with little shops and cafes; built on land owned by the Duke of Northumberland, the terminal arch bears the Coat of Arms of the Duke of York *(of 10,000 men fame)*

DID HOLLYWOOD START HERE?! No 7 The Corridor was the studio of William Friese-Green, the inventor of cinematography. Out of this alleyway came Pinewood..... and Hollywood!

THE LAURA FOUNTAIN splashes at the head of long, wide Great Pulteney Street.

GREAT PULTENEY STREET

100 feet wide, 1,000 feet long, Great Pulteney St is spectacular indeed. Used as a starting point for vintage car rallies, it's scale and grandeur reflect the elegance of Bath's Georgian era. The street is named after William Pulteney who owned and inspired the development of this grazing land, although it was his daughter Henrietta Laura who commissioned Thomas Baldwin the City Architect to design the street.

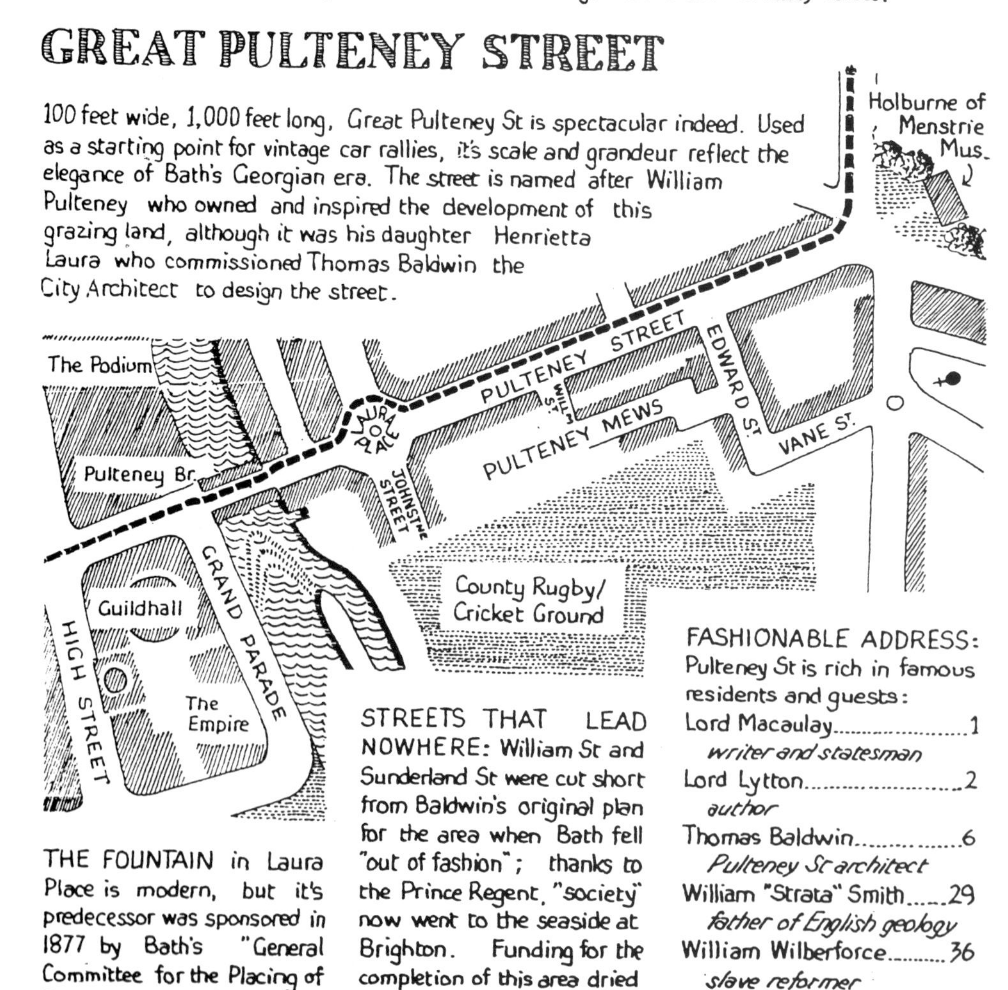

THE FOUNTAIN in Laura Place is modern, but it's predecessor was sponsored in 1877 by Bath's "General Committee for the Placing of Fountains in the City"

STREETS THAT LEAD NOWHERE: William St and Sunderland St were cut short from Baldwin's original plan for the area when Bath fell "out of fashion"; thanks to the Prince Regent, "society" now went to the seaside at Brighton. Funding for the completion of this area dried up.

FASHIONABLE ADDRESS: Pulteney St is rich in famous residents and guests:

- Lord Macaulay .... 1 — *writer and statesman*
- Lord Lytton .... 2 — *author*
- Thomas Baldwin .... 6 — *Pulteney St architect*
- William "Strata" Smith .... 29 — *father of English geology*
- William Wilberforce .... 36 — *slave reformer*
- Napolean III 55

...and the famous buildings at each end....

9 CROSS THE RIVER using Pulteney Bridge and walk - or "Parade" - the length of Great Pulteney Street. This is architecture on a grand scale, perhaps Bath's most noble, most expansive and most ambitious thoroughfare - the whole street and the vistas which close each end designed by Baldwin to impress you as one unified entity. Georgian Bath at its *most* grand.

PULTENEY BRIDGE *above* was originally conceived by William Pulteney, who needed a river crossing as the first stage of his plan to develop grazing land across the river in Bathwick. Pulteney's wealth enabled him to ask Robert Adam, a fellow Scot and the most fashionable architect of the 1770's, to design this magnificent bridge, which he did, possibly basing it on Palladio's unrealised design for the Ponte di Rialto in Venice. The result - completed in 1774 - is unique: three graceful arches, set above a sparkling weir, and England's only bridge supporting shops on both sides of the road. And what a delightful range of shops too, selling food, chocolates, crystal, stamps,...

THE HOLBURNE OF MENSTRIE MUSEUM crowns the view up Great Pulteney St. Designed by C. Harcourt Masters in 1795 as a pavilion for Sydney Gardens, it has been since then both a hydropathic hospital and a private school before assuming it's current role as a classical museum. It houses a remarkable collection of Old Master paintings by Gainsborough and Stubbs, silver and porcelain, plus a craft school. Entry attracts a small fee.

SYDNEY GARDENS

THE HEXAGONAL ENCLOSURE OF SYDNEY GARDENS *(see map below)* must rank as one of England's most complete family parks. Handsomely laid out parkland vies with children's playgrounds, tennis courts, a bowling green and, for transport lovers, both the Kennet and Avon Canal and the main London - Bath railway line run through the gardens.

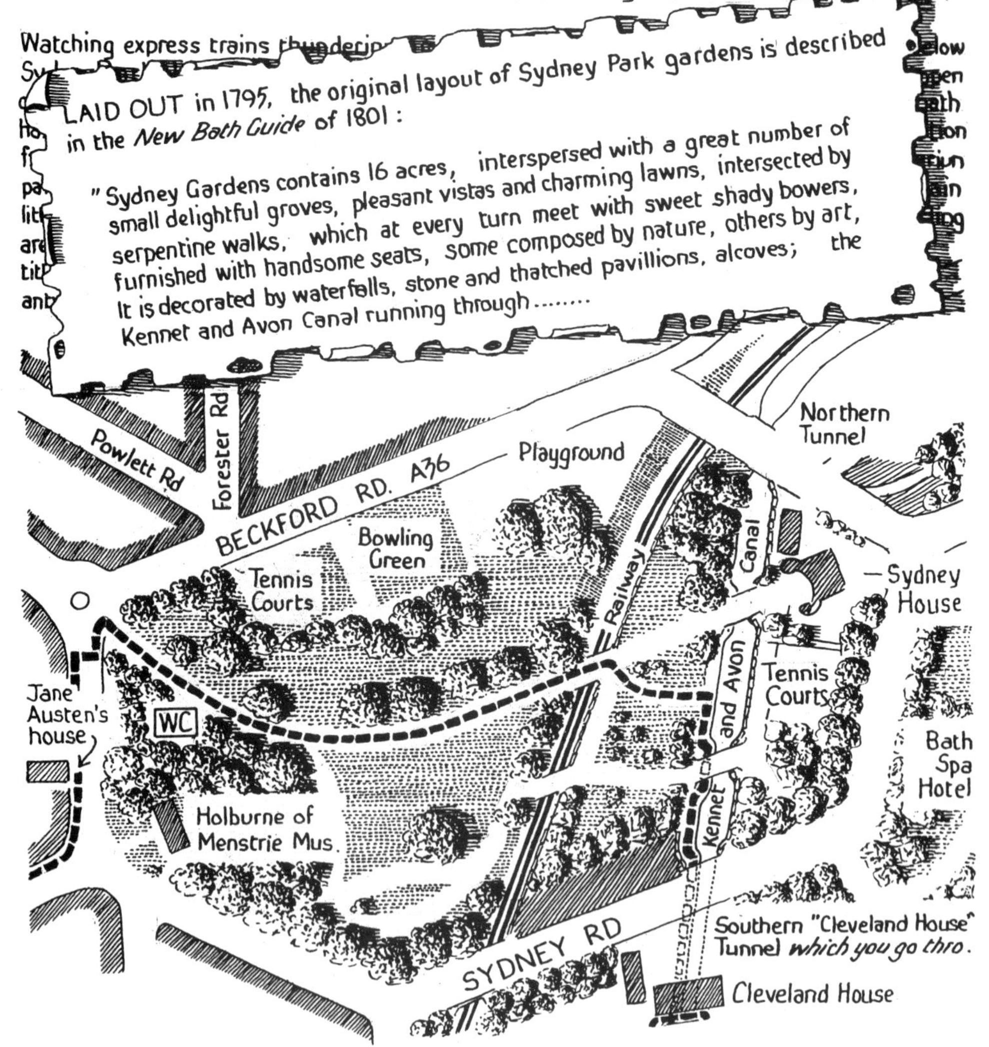

Watching express trains
LAID OUT in 1795, the original layout of Sydney Park gardens is described in the *New Bath Guide* of 1801 :
" Sydney Gardens contains 16 acres, interspersed with a great number of small delightful groves, pleasant vistas and charming lawns, intersected by serpentine walks, which at every turn meet with sweet shady bowers, furnished with handsome seats, some composed by nature, others by art, It is decorated by waterfalls, stone and thatched pavillions, alcoves; the Kennet and Avon Canal running through........
Powlett Rd
Forester Rd
BECKFORD RD. A36
Playground
Northern Tunnel
Bowling Green
Tennis Courts
Railway
Canal
Sydney House
Kennet and Avon
Tennis Courts
Jane Austen's house
WC
Bath Spa Hotel
Holburne of Menstrie Mus.
SYDNEY RD
Southern "Cleveland House" Tunnel *which you go thro.*
Cleveland House

10 AT THE TOP OF GREAT PULTENEY STREET turn left into Sydney Place to see Jane Austen's house .

11 CROSS THE *BUSY* ROAD into Sydney Park.....

12 HEAD FOR THE KENNET AND AVON CANAL which passes through the park, and once on the towpath, turn right.......

THE RAILWAY LINE through Sydney Gardens.....

A MODERN 125 TRAIN thunders through Sydney Park. The first train ran between London and Bath on 30 June 1841 after Brunel had engineered a railway through, and in complete harmony with, this lovely park. The ambience is wonderful!

......and Sydney Garden's most famous resident.......

4 SYDNEY PLACE was the home of the Austen family, whose famous literary daughter, Jane (1775-1817), wrote extensively about Bath in her novels *Northanger Abbey* and *Persuasion*. Jane Austen's famous association with Bath is somewhat ironic, because she actually disliked the place, finding the etiquette of Georgian high society very superficial when compared to the rural Hampshire village from whence she came. But, the many streets and buildings about which she wrote still stand, and many visitors enjoy guided "Jane Austen tours" of the City.

A walk along the Kennet and Avon Canal

13 THE KENNET AND AVON CANAL was cut through the privately owned Sydney Park in 1798 with agreed compensation of 2,000 guineas, plus "beautification" – two ornate wrought iron bridges and protective tunnels at either end.

14 CLEVELAND HOUSE, above the Southern Tunnel, was built for Henry, Duke of Cleveland, in 1825, then became the HQ of the Canal Company; a hole which still exists in the roof of the tunnel was used to pass bills from the offices above to the barges below!

15 TURNOVER BRIDGE: the towpath switches sides without the need to unhitch the horse. *Quite clever, really!*

16 SYDNEY WHARF – now a leisure boatyard – was once the commercial heart of Bath's thriving canal trade. At its peak in 1838 the canal bore 341,000 tonnes of freight.

17 NINE MILE POUND was the local name for the 9 mile stretch of canal from Top Lock to the next lock at Devizes. From Top Lock the canal rapidly falls the 60 feet to the level of the River Avon below, using 6 locks numbered 13 through to 7.

BESIDE WIDCOMBE LOCK was one of two pumping stations which reclaimed the large water loss when the locks were busy.

18 ALLENS WHARF – around locks 8/9 was the terminus of a 1½ mile horse drawn railway which brought Bathstone down from Ralph Allen's famous Combe Down Quarry.

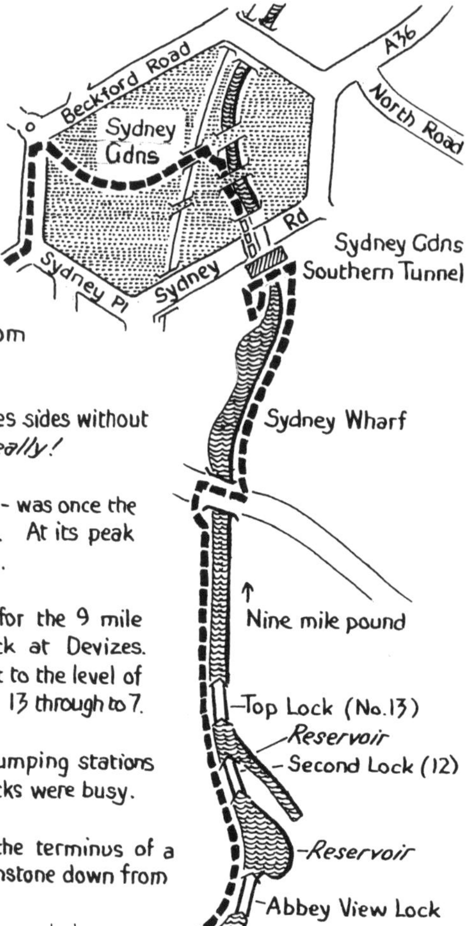

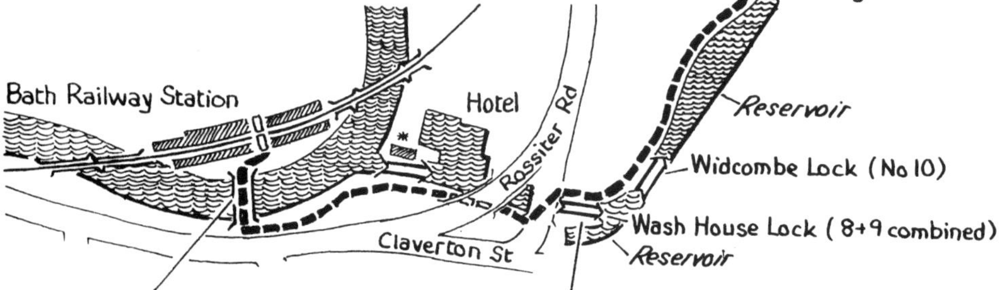

TRAGIC FOOTBRIDGE – cross the river on the footbridge called "½d bridge" – which replaces a wooden cantilever toll bridge which collapsed in 1877, killing 11 people queueing to pay their halfpenny toll.

ENGLAND'S DEEPEST LOCK road improvements led to the awesome combination of locks 8 and 9 to give what was, for a time, Englands deepest canal lock. Water level rise: 19'5".

*THIMBLE MILL (now a restaurant) was a pumping station reclaiming lost canal water by the lock full.

ENGLAND'S DEEPEST LOCK
LONDON ROAD A4
River Avon
Railway
Kennet and Avon Canal
WARMINSTER ROAD A36
BATHWICK ST
BECKFD RD
SYDNEY PL
GT PULT. ST
PULTENEY RD
BATH
Cleveland House Tunnel (14)
Top Lock, at the summit of a 20 metre *(60ft)* ascent from the River Avon
AVON CANAL
THE KE
opened in 181
nect the River
Kennet at Newbury with the River
Avon here in Bath. 86 miles long,
it bears 105 locks, 6 of which you are
about to explore *(numbers 7-13)* !
For 141 years the canal provided a
key trade link between the great ports
of Bristol and London, but eventually
closed in 1951, unable to compete with
the railways. Happily it reopened in
1990, thanks to volunteer effort.

BATH IN 1735.....

Adapted from John Wood's 1735 survey of Bath

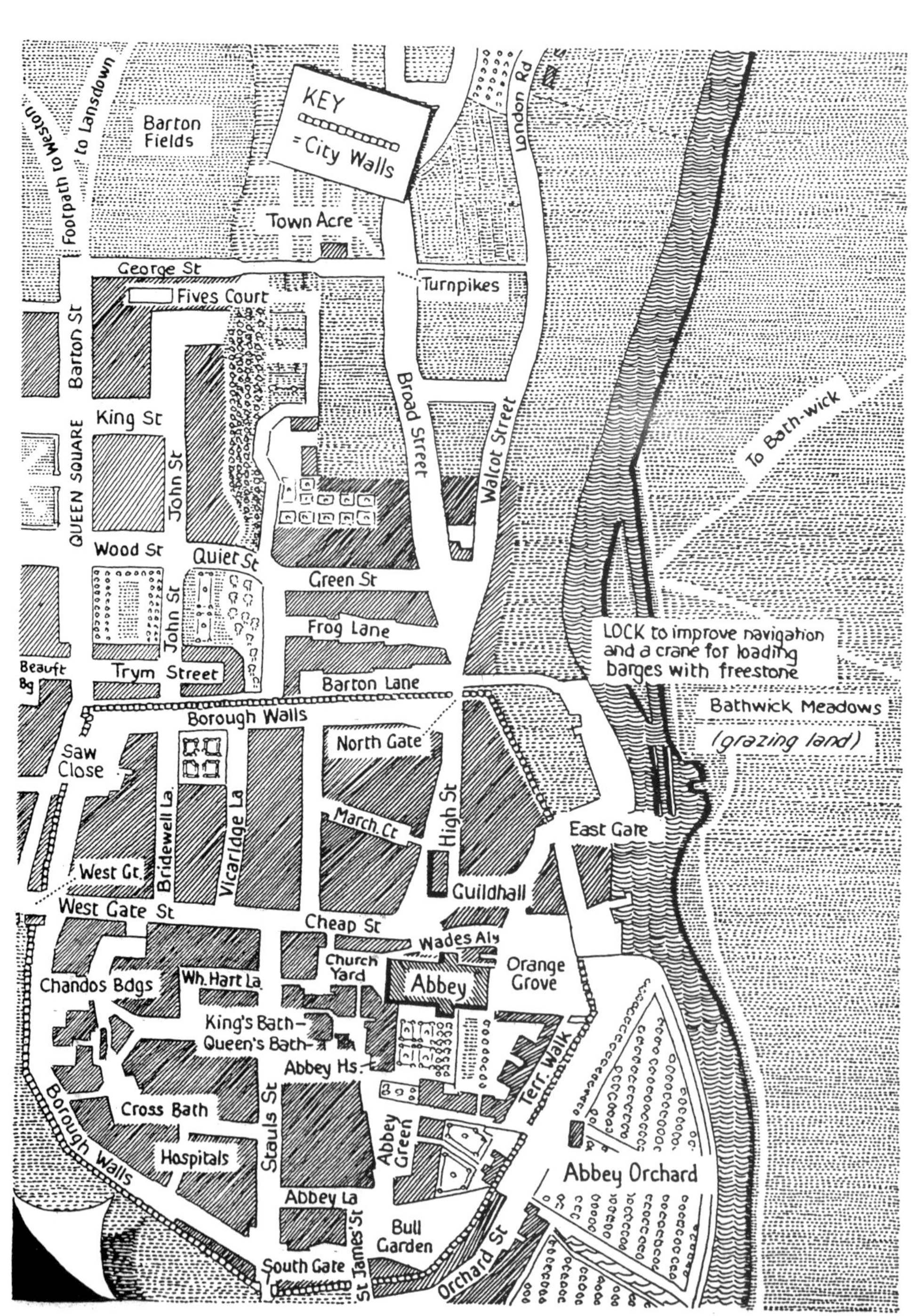

......AND THE SAME MAP, TODAY

THE MAP ON THE LEFT shows central Bath in 1735; the map on this page is of the same area but is up to date. You are about to walk through the mapped area - the oldest part of Bath.

In 1735, the Georgian revival of Bath was just beginning. The dissolution of the monasteries two centuries before had rendered the warm spa Baths more accessible to the public, and word had spread. The visit of Princess Anne in 1692, and her return as Queen in 1702/3 had kick started Bath's conversion into one of Europe's most elegant Cities. Already, as the map shows, Bath was full of formal gardens, theatres and halls.

The old map of Bath contains so much that is fascinating. Note that the City is still largely contained within it's city wall, and surrounded by pastureland. To the north, John Wood the Elder has completed Queen Sq., but not yet the Circus. To the east, Bathwick is still undeveloped meadow, owned by the Pulteney family. Throughout the town there are facets which are the precursors to what stands today. Browse on!!

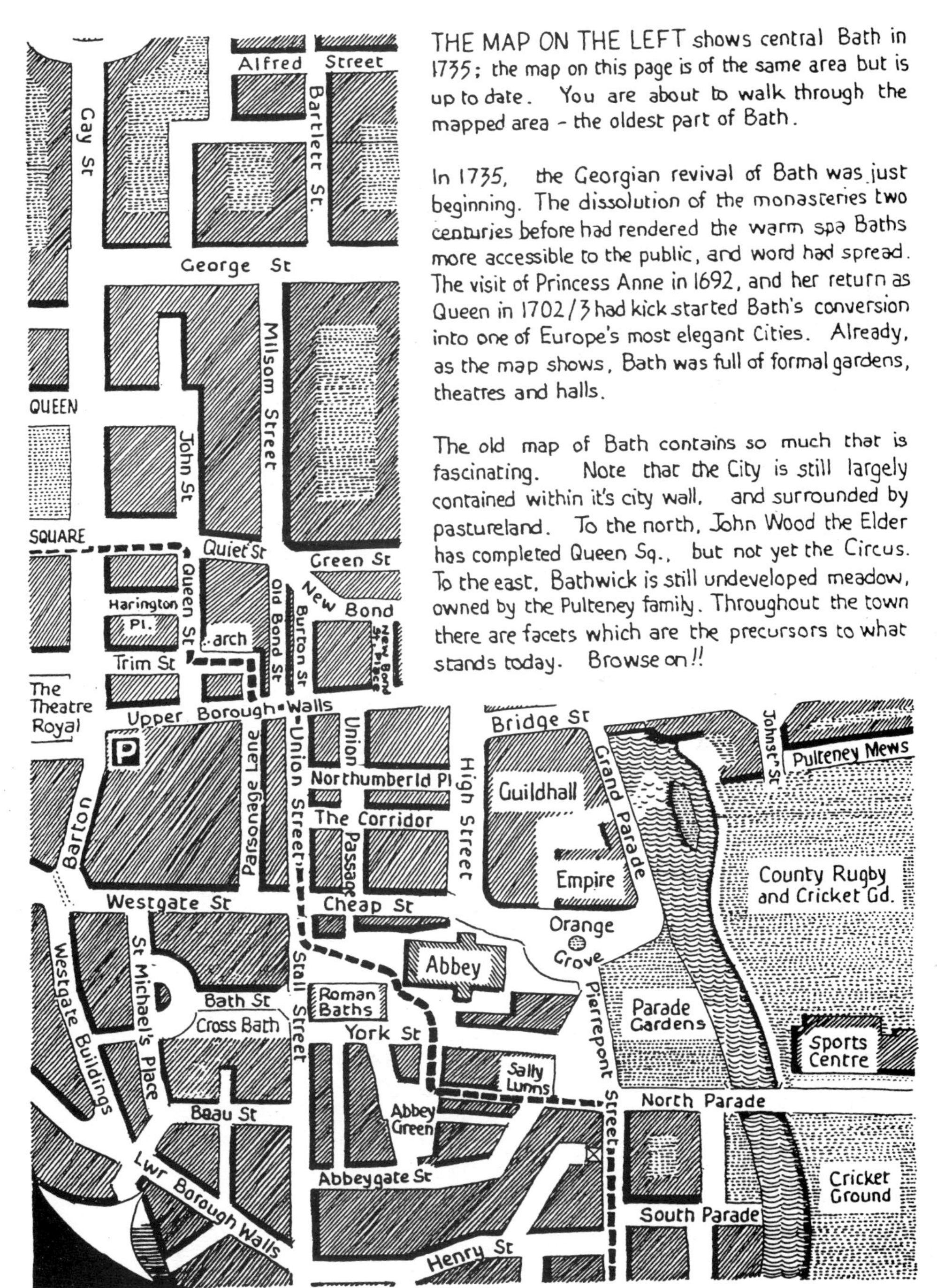

II NORTH PARADE was the home of Oliver Goldsmith (1728 - 1774) the Irish poet famed for his play *'She Stoops to Conquer'*

LADY HAMILTON lived at Linley House in Pierrepont Place, until she married the British Ambassador to Italy, then became Nelson's lover.

ADMIRAL LORD NELSON (1758 - 1805) - 88 Pierrepont St, died in victory fighting the French fleet at the Battle of Trafalgar

PIERREPONT STREET

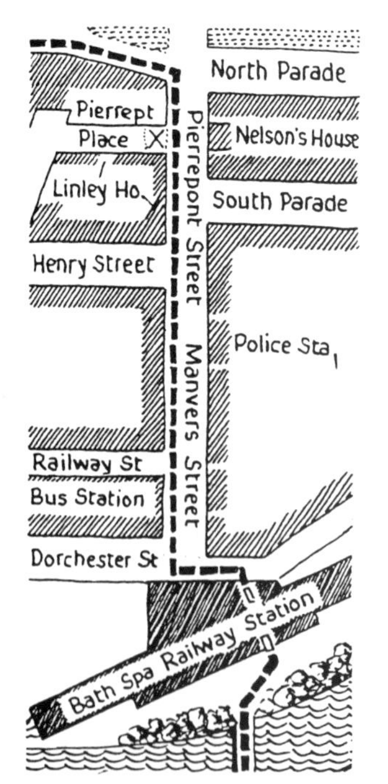

LOVE STORY: Through the tunnel into Pierrepont Place leads one to Linley House, one time home of the Linley family whose beautiful daughter Elizabeth eloped with the famous playright Sheridan in one of the classic 18th century love stories. Sheridan was not seen as a suitable match by Elizabeth's influential parents, so the two lovers plotted their escape by dead of night, arranging to travel via London to France where they were married. On their return Sheridan was forced to fight two duels against Elizabeth's other suitor - Captain Matthews - during the second of which he was injured. Elizabeth nursed Sheridan back to health, and he went on to to become one of the 18th century's most extrovert playwrights with comedies such as *The Rivals* and *School for Scandal.*

South Parade looking towards Pierrepont Street.....

THE WIDE PAVEMENT on South Parade enabled rich and fashionable Georgian ladies to "parade" - to walk, meet their friends and show off their finery.

AERIAL TRANSPORT: A train (→) pulls out of Bath Spa station for Bristol Temple Meads; such was the difficulty faced by Brunel when designing Bath's railway line in 1840, that he had to elevate it's entire run through the city, including the station, which is partly built on Skew Bridge

And a sightseeing bus(←), parked outside the bus - station in Manvers St.; omnibus tours of Bath's main sights are popular with the City's two million visitors each year - esp. on the top deck!

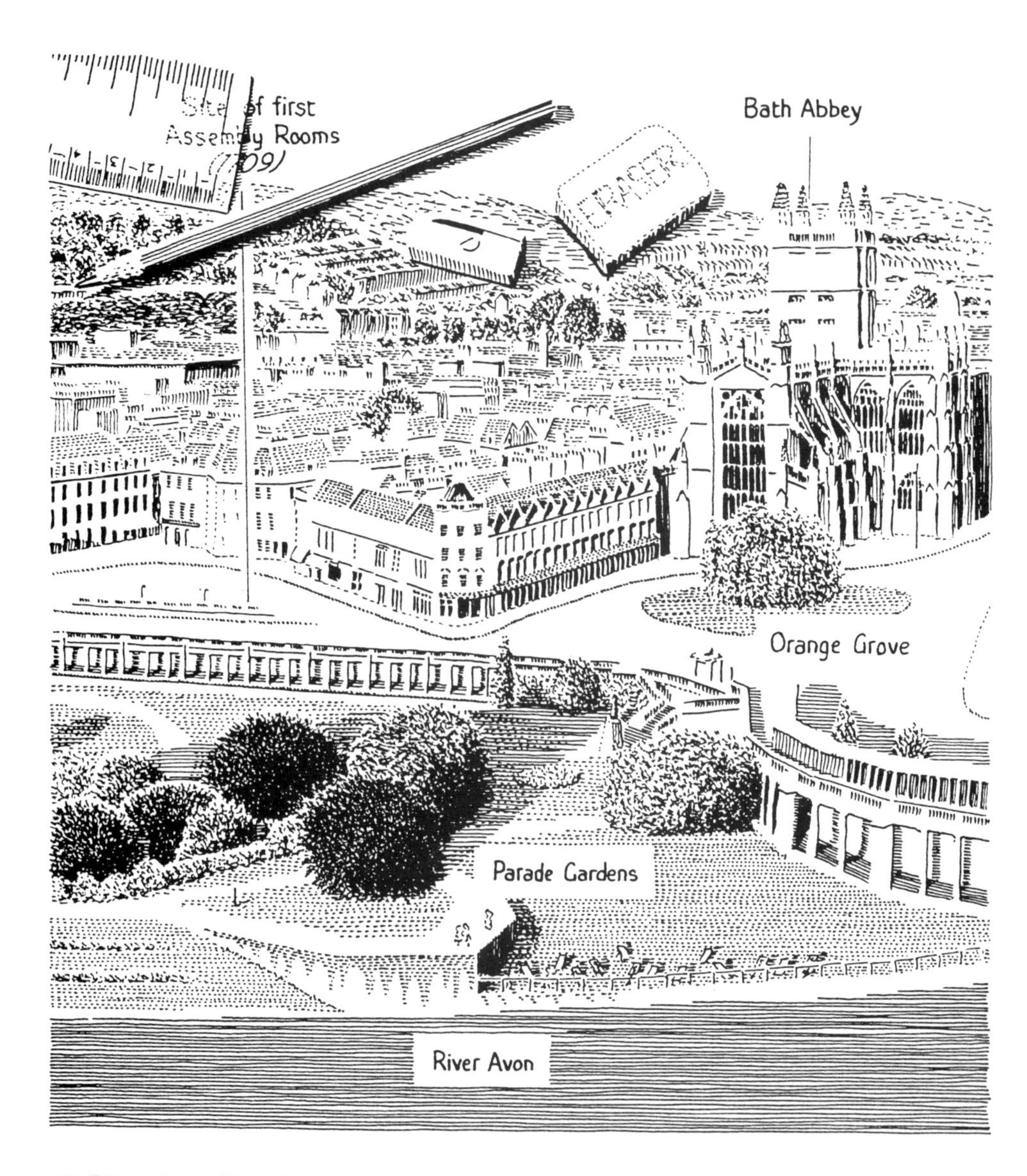

ORANGE GROVE

OVERLOOKING the River Avon and with lovely views across the valley towards Ralph Allens "Sham Castle", Orange Grove is a busy junction for Bath City centre traffic. The terraced walk above the Colonnade overlooks Parade Gardens *(pictured above)* - a pleasant sanctuary in which the Bath Parks Department puts on a commendable floral display every summer; indeed, a series of plaques on Parade Steps commemorate Baths frequent victories in the "Britain in Bloom" contest

From the Gardens take the formal walk along the Colonnade, which follows the riverside to Pulteney Weir. Built in 1971 to protect the City from floods, the sight, sound and drama of the sparkling waterfall from close by are unforgetable. The Poet Laureat Sir John Betjeman gloried in this view – and I recommend that you do too! An experience not to be missed!

VICTORIAN LANDMARK: The Empire Hotel, completed in 1901, was commandeered as Admiralty HQ during World War II, but is now prestigious flats. The architect, C.E.Davis, designed it's skyline to show the three levels of English society:

castle
the nobility

ornamented gable
middle class

cottage
artisan

ACROSS THE RIVER: County Rugby Ground

Discovering BATH
MAP OF THE WALK

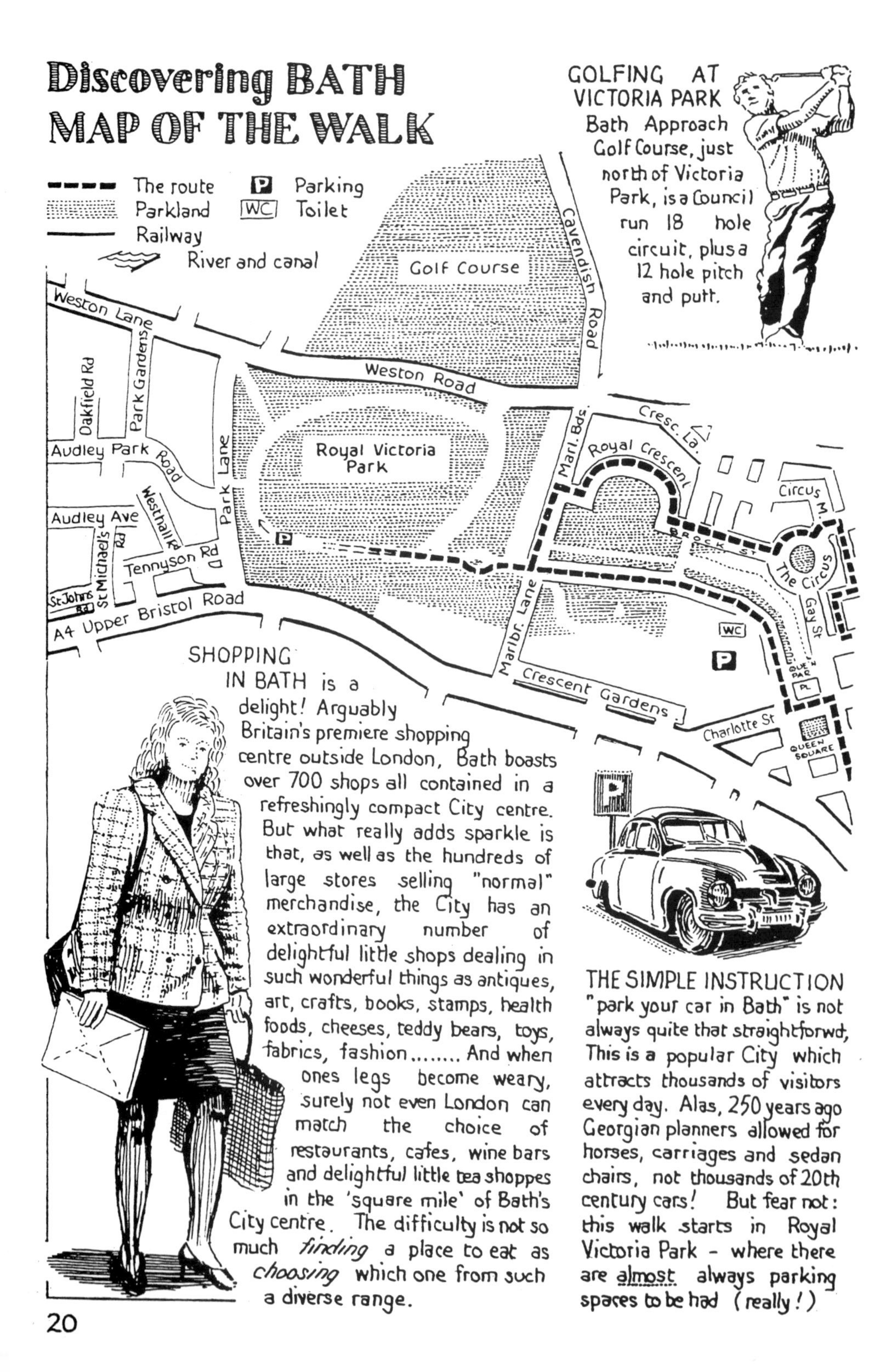

GOLFING AT VICTORIA PARK

Bath Approach Golf Course, just north of Victoria Park, is a Council run 18 hole circuit, plus a 12 hole pitch and putt.

SHOPPING IN BATH is a delight! Arguably Britain's premiere shopping centre outside London, Bath boasts over 700 shops all contained in a refreshingly compact City centre. But what really adds sparkle is that, as well as the hundreds of large stores selling "normal" merchandise, the City has an extraordinary number of delightful little shops dealing in such wonderful things as antiques, art, crafts, books, stamps, health foods, cheeses, teddy bears, toys, fabrics, fashion........ And when ones legs become weary, surely not even London can match the choice of restaurants, cafes, wine bars and delightful little tea shoppes in the 'square mile' of Bath's City centre. The difficulty is not so much *finding* a place to eat as *choosing* which one from such a diverse range.

THE SIMPLE INSTRUCTION "park your car in Bath" is not always quite that straightforwd, This is a popular City which attracts thousands of visitors every day. Alas, 250 years ago Georgian planners allowed for horses, carriages and sedan chairs, not thousands of 20th century cars! But fear not: this walk starts in Royal Victoria Park - where there are almost always parking spaces to be had (really!)

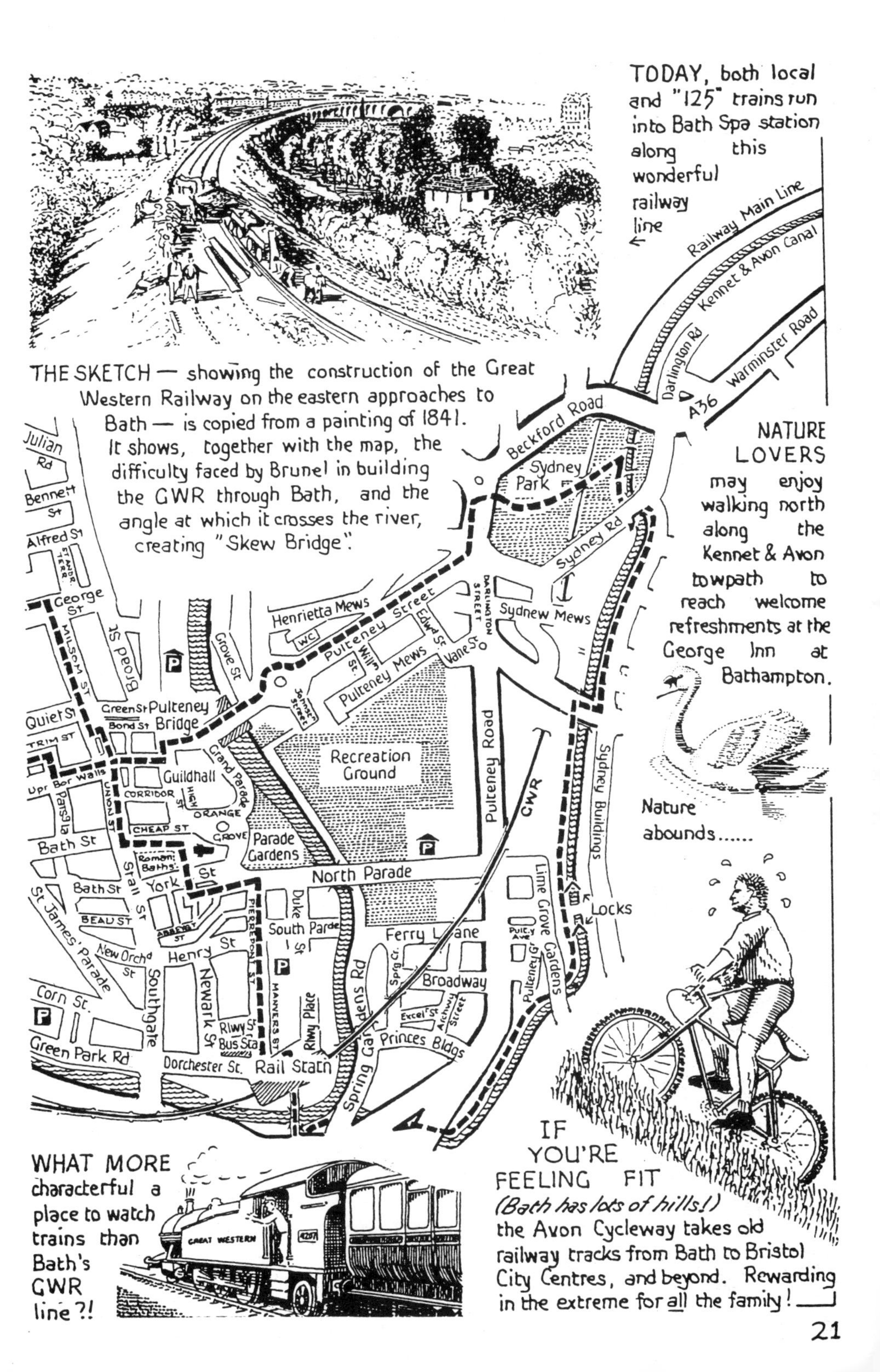

TODAY, both local and "125" trains run into Bath Spa station along this wonderful railway line
THE SKETCH — showing the construction of the Great Western Railway on the eastern approaches to Bath — is copied from a painting of 1841. It shows, together with the map, the difficulty faced by Brunel in building the GWR through Bath, and the angle at which it crosses the river, creating "Skew Bridge".
NATURE LOVERS may enjoy walking north along the Kennet & Avon towpath to reach welcome refreshments at the George Inn at Bathampton.
Nature abounds......
WHAT MORE characterful a place to watch trains than Bath's GWR line ?!
GREAT WESTERN
IF YOU'RE FEELING FIT
(Bath has lots of hills!)
the Avon Cycleway takes old railway tracks from Bath to Bristol City Centres, and beyond. Rewarding in the extreme for all the family!
Railway Main Line
Kennet & Avon Canal
Darlington Rd
Warminster Road
A36
Beckford Road
Sydney Park
Sydney Rd
Julian Rd
Bennett St
Alfred St
George St
Milsom St
Broad St
Grove St
Henrietta Mews
Pulteney Street
Edwd St
Darlington Street
Sydnew Mews
Vane St
Pulteney Mews
Johnson Street
WC
Green St
Pulteney Bridge
Quiet St
Bond St
Trim St
Grand Parade
Recreation Ground
Pulteney Road
GWR
Sydney Buildings
Upr Bor Walls
Guildhall
Corridor
Union St
High St
Orange Grove
Cheap St
Bath St
Parade Gardens
Roman Baths
York St
North Parade
Lime Grove Gardens
Locks
Stall St
Bath St
Beau St
Abbey St
Pierrepont St
Duke St
South Parade
Ferry Lane
St James' Parade
New Orchd St
Henry St
Southgate
Newark St
Manvers St
Rlwy Place
Spring Gardens Rd
Sprg Cr.
Broadway
Pulteney Gr
Corn St.
Rlwy St
Bus Sta
Excel St
Archway Street
Princes Bldgs
Green Park Rd
Dorchester St.
Rail Statn

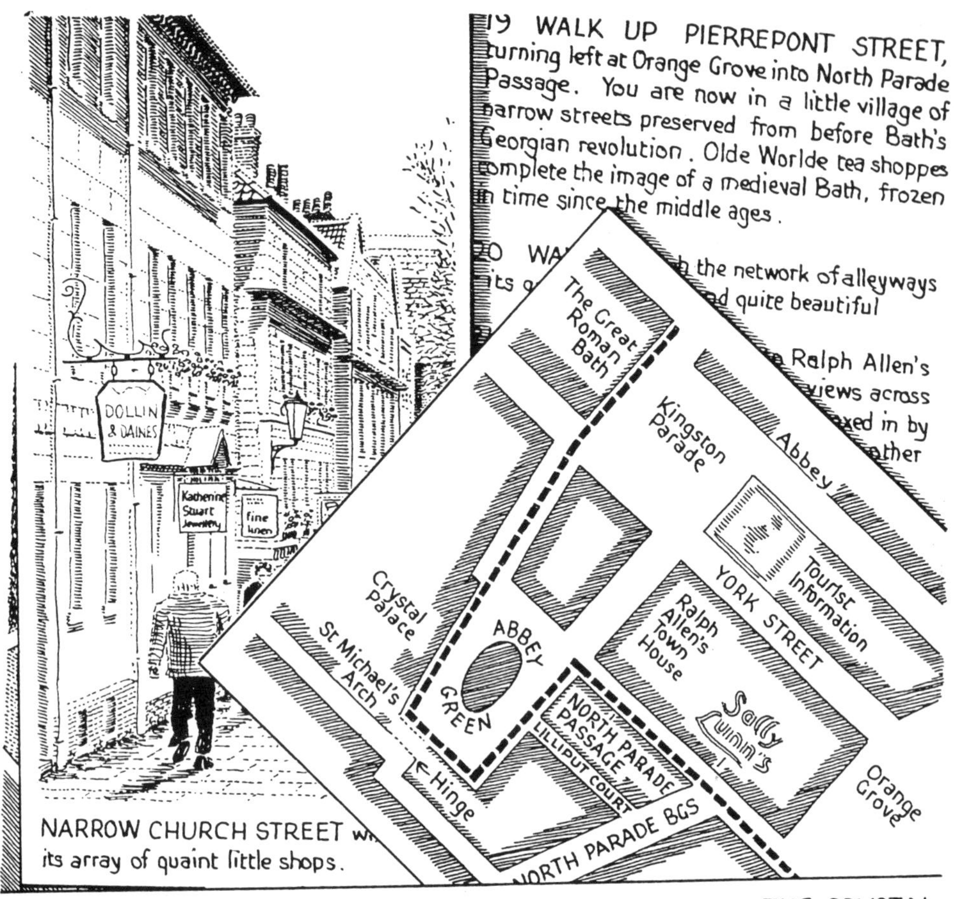

19 WALK UP PIERREPONT STREET, turning left at Orange Grove into North Parade Passage. You are now in a little village of narrow streets preserved from before Bath's Georgian revolution. Olde Worlde tea shoppes complete the image of a medieval Bath, frozen in time since the middle ages.

20 WA... h the network of alleyways its a... d quite beautiful

... Ralph Allen's ... views across ... xed in by ... ather

NARROW CHURCH STREET w... its array of quaint little shops.

THE CRYSTAL PALACE was the convalescent home of Admiral Lord Nelson after being wounded in the Battle of the Nile in 1798. Its more recent name is in honour of the Great Exhibition Centre of 1851.

A 2nd century Roman mosaic has been unearthed below the cellars of the Crystal Palace pub.

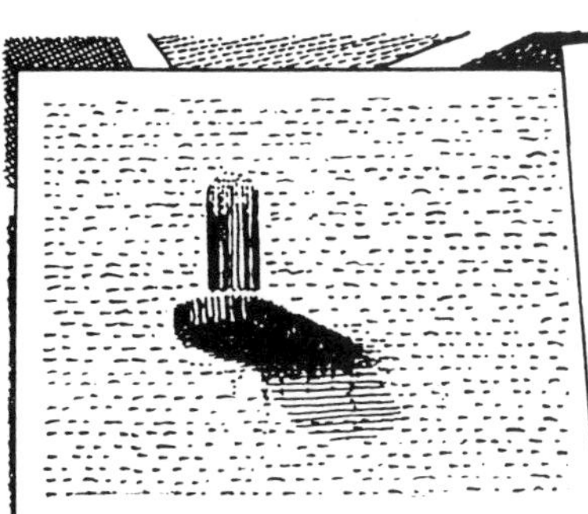

A HINGE set into the wall of St Michael's Arch forms the last remnant of the once great Abbey Gardens. Bath Abbey once dominated the City occupying a quarter of the area inside the medieval walls; this hinge supported its huge south gate. Reformation in the 16th century, combined with dissolution by Henry VIII spelt the end of the Abbeys grip on the City, and in the 1570s the Abbey Gardens were sold into privat[...] Only the hi[...]

PRE-GEORGIAN BATH

ABBEY GREEN *(pictured right)* is a wonderfully peaceful little oasis in the centre of Bath's pre-Georgian area, utterly dominated by a huge London Plane tree, dating back to the old Abbey Gardens. The archway in the South West corner *(see picture)* was sympathetically built by Marks & Spencers at the same time as their new store next door.

SALLY LUNN'S HOUSE on North Parade Passage, built in 1482, is reputedly the oldest house in Bath.

Sally Lunn was a Huguenot refugee who brought from France the recipe for brioche. In 1680 she opened a bakery here and her buns - based on her French recipe - won immediate acclaim from the high society of the day. Then, as now tea at Sally Lunn's was a part of the culture of Bath - a local luxury which has stood the enduring test of time for 300 yrs.

Sally Lunn, however, was not the first person to prepare food here; excavations in 1989 revealed a medieval faggot oven, and two metres below the cellar the floor of the original Roman house has been unearthed. The basement - which was the ground floor in pre - Georgian times - has been turned into an interesting museum which is well worth an educational visit.

STREET LEVEL IN Central Bath was raised by one complete storey during the Georgian redevelopment of the City. Thus this view of Sally Lunn's actually starts not from the *ground* floor but from the original *first* floor. Central Bath has many other clues to this raised street level including Parade Gardens, Ralph Allen's town house off York St, and the little cafes in Pre-Georgian Bath.

ONE OF BATH'S MOST SPECIAL VIEWS awaits you as you emerge from Pre-Georgian Bath. The wide open space of Kingston Parade, with Bath Abbey towering behind. To the right is the Tourist Inform'tn Centre - always well worth a visit if you want to know whats going on in Bath; to the left are the Roman Baths. In the middle, surrounded by a quadrant of chairs, a street entertainer sings to the crowds; in an hours time he could be replaced by a clown, or a juggler, or a classical musician.

And because most visitors stay at the *front* of the Abbey, and this is round the *side*, we find there is always a seat free here to rest weary legs.

Kingston Parade: a great place to stop awhile and rest.

RESTFUL PLACES TO STOP AWHILE

OF EVEN GREATER INTEREST is what lies below Kingston Parade. 6 metres underneath the paving lie the Roman East Baths - excavated and open to view - a network of hot + cold baths known as the Lucas Bath, the Tepidarium and the Caldarium.

THE FOUNDER BISHOP OLIVER'S DREAM of Angels ascending and descending from heaven is depicted in Bath Abbey's famous West front carvings.

BATH ABBEY

EDGAR, King of Wessex from 959, was crowned the 1st King of a united England at Bath Abbey in 973. An all powerful King, he is creditted with setting up law courts, reforming the wayward monasteries and bringing peace to a troubled nation. Upon his death just 2 years later, aged only 32, England once again fell into confusion, which was to last until 1066.

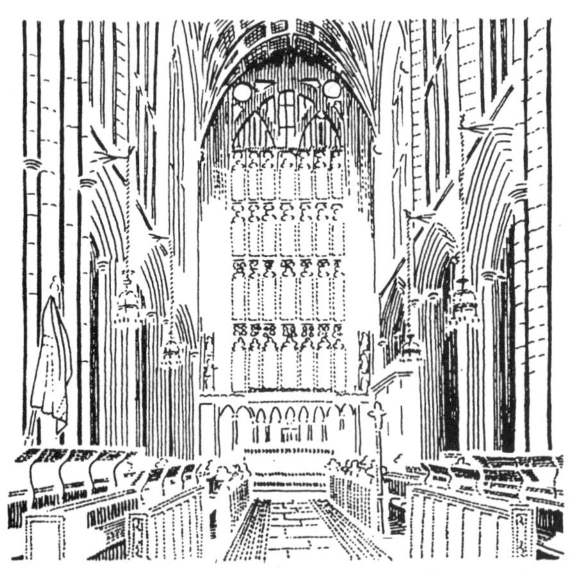

INSIDE, the great east window contains 56 scenes from the life of Christ, and has been restored from damage suffered during World War II.

"THE LANTERN OF THE WEST" is a very fitting Elizabethan description of Bath Abbey. Its *huge* area of glass in its clerestory windows, the sheer height of its fan vaulting - *78ft above the floor* - and its massive 162ft tower all fill one with awe. Steeply sloping flying buttresses along the length of the nave and chancel, and the tall slender windows of the transepts, add considerably to the effect. *The illustration below demonstrates all these features........*

THIS IS THE THIRD GREAT CHURCH to be built on this site. A Saxon Abbey in 781 was replaced by a Norman Cathedral in 1107. Something of the importance of the medieval Abbey is shown by Edgar's coronation here as the first King of a united England in 973. But it was in a legendary dream that the then Bishop of Bath and Wells, Oliver King, was inspired to build the current, huge Abbey in 1499. In his dream, Oliver saw angels on a ladder connecting heaven with earth, the Holy Trinity, and an olive tree, on which rested a crown. A heavenly voice told him to restore the Cathedral, which he set about organising. The West Front depicts the story of his dream, showing the angels on the ladders, olive trees and the Trinity..

A brief history of Bath......

THE MAGIC OF HOT SPRING WATER

FLINT AXES unearthed during recent excavations show that the marvel of hot water bubbling from the ground has been attracting visitors to Bath for more than 8,000 years. For the hot springs of Bath *are* its history – a story of man's fascination.........

THE LEGENDARY FOUNDER of Bath was Bladud, a prince of ancient Britain in the 9th century BC. Banished from court because he bore an infectious skin disease, he became a swineherd on the banks of the River Avon. One day, he noticed that his pigs had also caught the disease, but when they bathed in the warm mud alongside the river they were cured. Thus, in 863BC the hot spa waters of Bath had healed their first patients. Pigs! It is to celebrate this legend that many Georgian buildings in Bath are decorated with acorns on their cornices.

Observing the pigs cure, Bladud dived into the warm mud as well, and was also cured; returning home, he eventually became King. Out of gratitude, Bladud set up his court in Bath. The 'City of Bath' had been founded.

Right: Bladud presides over the Hot Baths, as a statue carved in 1699.

THE GILDED BRONZE HEAD of Sulis-Minerva, unearthed whilst workmen dug under Stall St in 1727.

THE ROMANS FIRST CAME TO ENGLAND in AD43 and initially occupied only the fertile lands of the South East; their border was the nearby Fosse Way, and Bath was a small frontier fort.

But the Romans, as their forebears, held Hot Springs in religious awe; this was the place where they believed that their world met the mysterious underworld. The great city of Aquae Sulis soon arose, with their temple – dedicated to the goddess Sulis-Minerva *(see picture left)* at its centre.

Today, 2,000 years later, the advanced culture of this great Roman city is wonderfully displayed in the Roman museum under the Pump Room complex. Perhaps the most dramatic view of British ancient history you will find anywhere in Britain, the museum contains reconstructions, artefacts, mosaics and the actual Roman remains which were "Aquae Sulis"

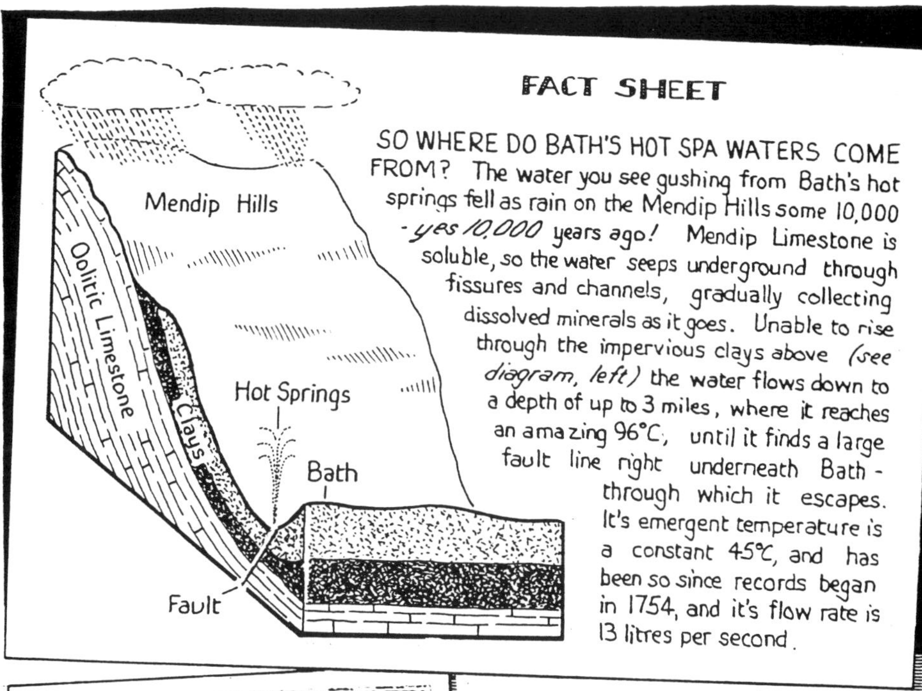

FACT SHEET

SO WHERE DO BATH'S HOT SPA WATERS COME FROM? The water you see gushing from Bath's hot springs fell as rain on the Mendip Hills some 10,000 - *yes 10,000* years ago! Mendip Limestone is soluble, so the water seeps underground through fissures and channels, gradually collecting dissolved minerals as it goes. Unable to rise through the impervious clays above *(see diagram, left)* the water flows down to a depth of up to 3 miles, where it reaches an amazing 96°C, until it finds a large fault line right underneath Bath - through which it escapes. It's emergent temperature is a constant 45°C, and has been so since records began in 1754, and it's flow rate is 13 litres per second.

THE ROMANS WERE MASTERS of hydraulic engineering, and left intact a water management system impressive even by modern standards. *Pictured above* is the overflow archway from the hot spring, which still serves its original purpose today, nearly 2,000 years later.

THE END OF THE ROMAN EMPIRE in the 5th century AD was slow and merciless; driven by raids of barbarians who took few prisoners, populations fled from the cities and Aquae Sulis fell into ruin.

England entered "the Dark Ages".

That "Bath" slowly re-emerged from the ruins of Aquae Sulis is proved by the existence of a small monastery here in 781, presumably attracted by the hot springs. It grew in importance, such that Edgar, the first King of a united England, was crowned here in 973 AD.

Henry VIII

Bath Abbey dominated the life of the City for the next 500 yrs in a prolonged period of monastic peace and stagnation. Its end was to be abrupt and monumental... thanks to Henry VIII.

THE SPA, and Bath's Georgian Revival

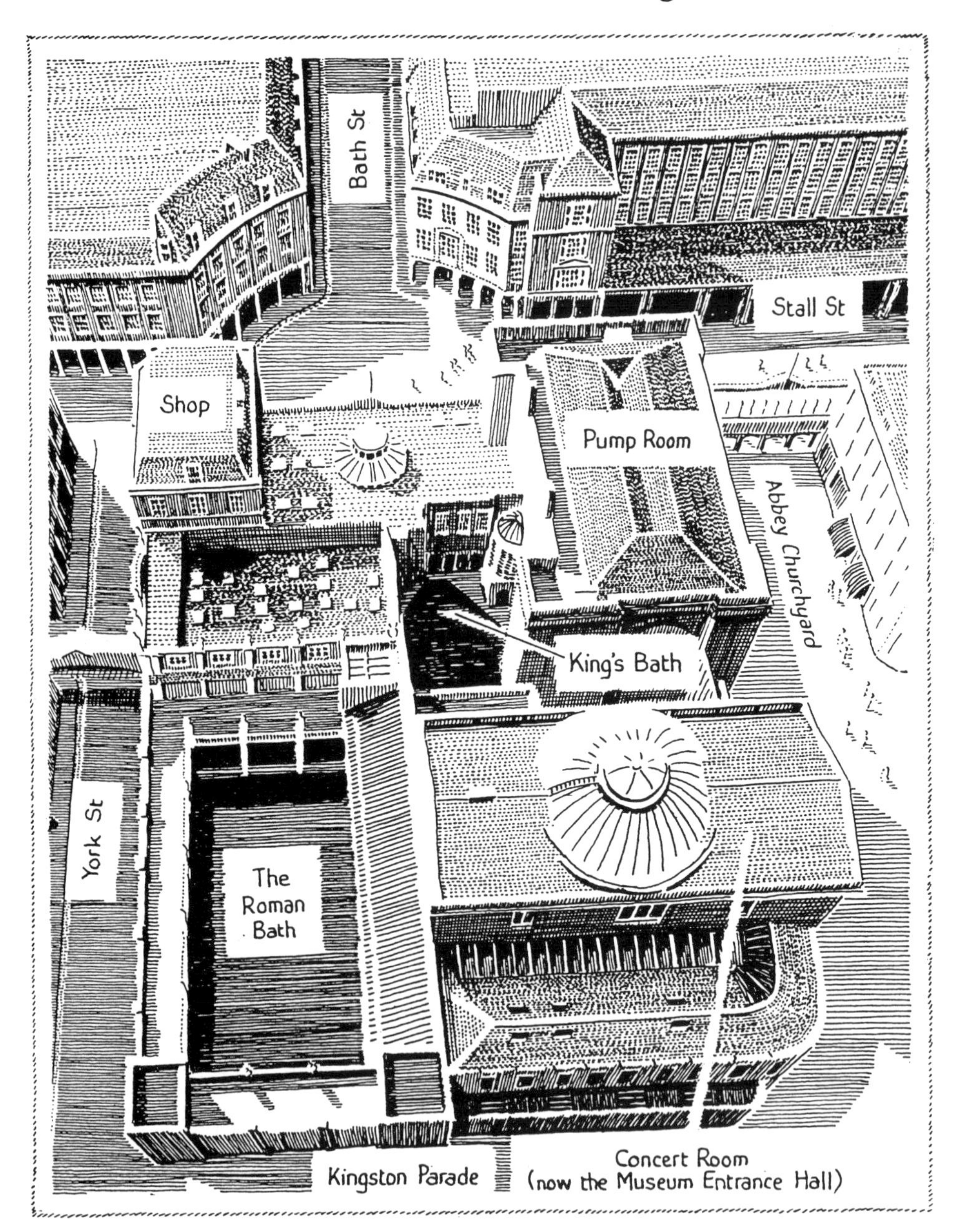

AN AERIAL VIEW OF THE SPA COMPLEX TODAY shows its two baths; the King's Bath lies directly over the sacred spring and has been in continuous use since Roman times. The Roman Baths, unbelievably hidden underground for more than a millenium, were excavated in Victorian times to form what you see today. Tea and Bath buns in the Pump Room is still one of England's great "civilised things to do" to the tones of the world's oldest music ensemble.

THE KING'S BATH in 1675, copied from a drawing by T Johnson

HENRY VIII dissolved Bath Abbey, along with 50 other monasteries, because they owed allegience to Rome; the Abbey was forced to release its grip over the City and the Hot Baths, and all public buildings passed to the Civic Authorities. Slowly, Bath absorbed a new entrepreneurial spirit, and crowds of visitors began to flock to Bath to be healed by the curative Spa waters. The revival of Bath had begun.......

IT WAS THE VISIT of Princess Anne in 1692, and her return as Queen in 1702 and 1703 which really kick started the revival of Bath. Where Royalty led, the aristocracy were never far behind, and within half a century Bath had become one of Europe's most elegant Cities. Money and society poured in; Bath was not only the place to be, but the place in which to be seen. Much of what you see in Bath today originates from this second heyday in the 18th century.

The Spa waters were drunk, rather than bathed in *'Roman style'*, and to this end the first pump room was built in 1706. As Bath's popularity grew a larger facility was required; the present Pump Room *(pictured right)* was completed in 1792 to resemble the Roman temple.

But, like Aquae Sulis before, it was not to last. In the early 19th century "society", led by the Prince Regent, started bathing in the sea at Brighton. Bath was no longer the most fashionable place to be.

THE PUMP ROOM viewed from its famous colonnade

ABBEY CHURCHYARD

AN EERIE CONNECTION links the two drawings above. On the right is the Abbey Churchyard as it appears today, a busy focus of Bath life. On the left is my impression of Roman Bath, 2 millenia ago, looking across the Precinct to the Temple of Sulis Minerva. The link is that both pictures are the same view, looking in the same direction from the same point ~ ⊛ on the map opposite.

After the Roman army had retreated from England in the 5th century the Baths complex fell into disuse and was gradually covered by several metres of sediment. "Bath" then developed without any apparent knowledge of the Roman ruins below.

THE GORGON'S HEAD looking down over the Roman precinct.

22 WALK ACROSS THE ABBEY CHURCHYARD then turn right into Stall Street.

THE ABBEY CHURCHYARD today. ↑

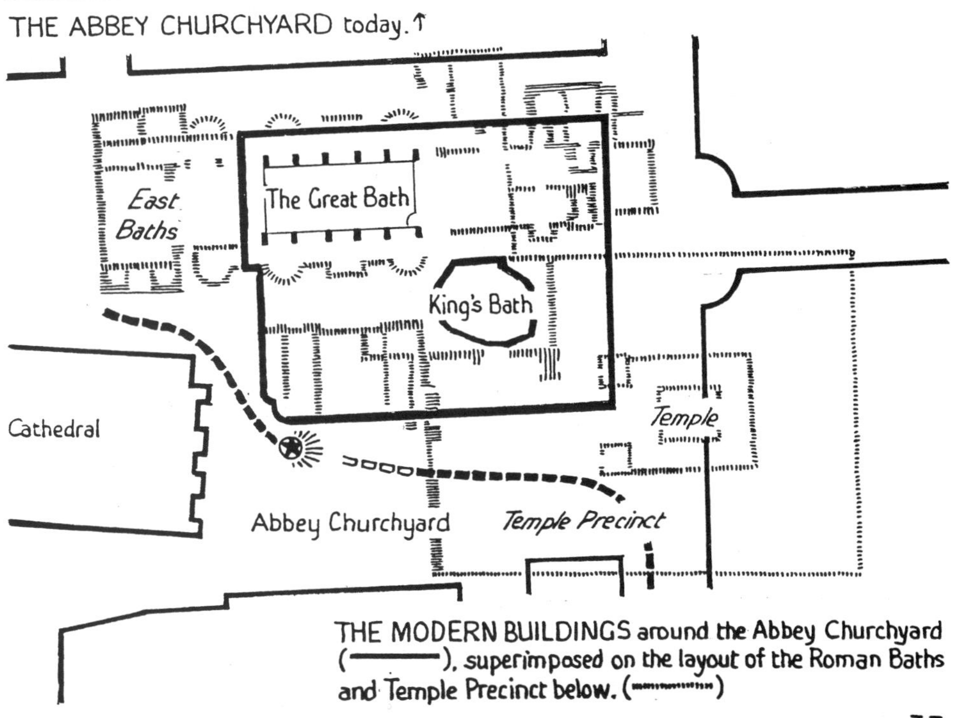

THE MODERN BUILDINGS around the Abbey Churchyard (———), superimposed on the layout of the Roman Baths and Temple Precinct below. (┉┉┉)

Lovely cheese shop
WOOD ST.
QUIET
Northumberl'd Buildings.
Harington Hotel
QUEEN STREET
HARINGTON PL.
BARTON ST.
Trim Bridge
General Wolfe's
TRIM STREET
Beau Nash's House
Popjoys
Theatre Royal
Ancient Walls
UPPER BOROUGH WALLS
Bluecoat School
PAR
Royal Mineral Wa
THROUGH TRIM BRIDGE into Queen St.; more correctly called St. John's Gate, this lovely archway was opened sometime after 1728 to provide access to Queen Square.
MINERVA Art Supplies
THE ANCIENT CITY WALLS are easily traced in Bath by following such street names as Terrace Walk, Lower and Upper Borough Walls, West, North and Southgate Streets. But only in Upper Borough Walls *(above)* does the last remaining stretch of the original wall survive, much restored, and built on Roman foundations.
Union Street
Stall Street
FIELD MARSHAL WADE'S HOUSE in Abbey Churchyard is now the National Trust Shop. Built in 1720, it is Bath's earliest house in the Palladian style
Field Marshal Wade's Hse
ABBEY CHURCHYARD

FROM WHERE IT ALL STARTED........

23 HEAD NORTH FROM STALL STREET through the maze of little streets towards Queen Square *(see map, left)* and you will walk through the area from where Bath's Georgian building boom first started. Field Marshal Wade's house *(see picture)* was Bath's first house to be built in the Palladian style which was to become the City's 'hallmark' for the next 100 years.

WOLFE'S HOUSE: 5 Trim St was the home of General Wolfe (1727-59), a brilliant military strategist who was sent from Bath to Canada to engage the French army at Quebec. He won a famous victory, routing the French in just 11 minutes, but, alas, the short battle cost him his life; Wolfe died of a musket wound on the Heights of Abraham. A famous painting of the dying hero, by Benjamin West, hangs in the National Gallery of Canada.

← IN PRAISE OF A TOILET! The Harington Hotel *(pictured left)* in Queen Street was named after the family of local landowners whose great forebear, Sir John Harington, godson of Queen Elizabeth I, is credited with the invention of the first flushing WC in 1596. His name - "John" - has been fondly associated with his invention ever since. A Bath man, a poet and a satirist, Sir John was also closely involved with Bath Abbey in its early years.

The windows in the Harington Hotel were bricked up to avoid paying Window taxes, levied from 1691 to 1851. Buildings with more than 6 windows were taxed.

FAMOUS INSTITUTIONS

AT EACH END OF UPPER BOROUGH WALLS stand the homes of two long established British social traditions.....

THE THEATRE ROYAL, Bath, *(pictured below)*, is a playhouse of national importance being - in 1767 - the first outside London to gain the Royal Charter. Two centuries later its programme still includes a wealth of fascinating plays, comedies and Christmas pantomimes.

BUT THE THEATRE COMPLEX has a fascinating history of its own predating its conversion to a playhouse in 1805. It was originally the house of Richard "Beau" Nash, celebrated Master of Ceremonies for 50 years from 1705, and one of the three men thought responsible for turning Bath into a centre of Georgian fashion. Nash lived here with his mistress Juliana Popjoy, hence *"Popjoys"* - the name of the restaurant next door.

Nash's first house is now the Garrick's Head public house, on the left of the picture *above*, a famous meeting place for Bath's acting fraternity. Built in 1720, it was described by John Wood as the "Palace of the King of Bath... the richest sample of building executed in the City." Tradition has it that Nash lost this house to David Garrick - an actor - as a gambling debt. So Nash relocated a few houses to the North - the house just appearing on the right of the picture *above* - to live with his mistress until his death - penniless - in 1761. Juliana Popjoy was so affected by her lover's death that she is said to have lived her remaining years in a hollow tree.

200 YEARS BEFORE THE NHS: Bath's Royal Mineral Water Hospital *(pictured below)* was England's first to welcome patients on the basis of need, not ability to pay. The poor as well as the wealthy came here to be cured by "the waters".......

THE IDEA of founding a hospital for poor visitors coming to Bath who wished to be cured originated as early as 1716, but it took 20 years bot funds enough to be raised by public subscription. Eventually in 1742, amidst great celebrations, the hospital opened and *(pictured above)* survives to this day as the country's leading hospital for the treatment of rheumatic diseases.

BATH OLIVERS - hard, somewhat bland savoury biscuits, were invented by Dr Oliver, the chief physician at the Royal Mineral Water Hospital, to prescribe to patients who had eaten a little too well!! Still on sale in Bath today; they were Britain's first ever cream cracker biscuit!

When first built the hospital faced out over the City Walls *(see page 42)* to green fields and must have been an awe inspiring sight. The hospital cemetery was immediately over the wall adjoining Trim St - *outside* the City walls as required of local byelaws.

QUEEN SQUARE

THE FRANCIS, which forms the South side of Queen Square, combines 6 houses to form one sumptuous 95 bedroom hotel. Coffee here *(a welcome relief after a lengthy shopping trip!)*, gives an insight into the elegant interiors of Wood's buildings. Built in 1728, the top two storeys housed the large quota of household servants.

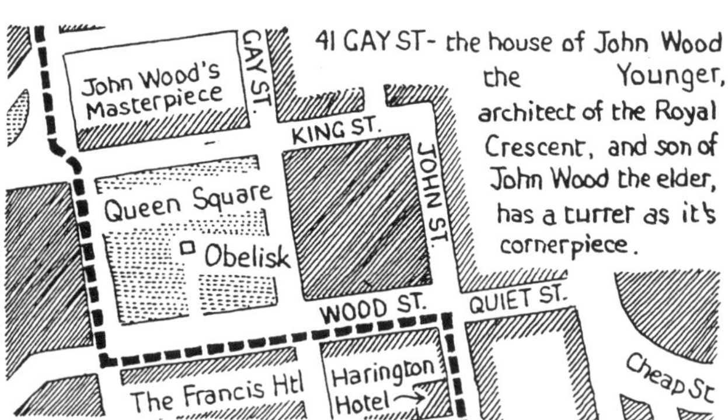

41 GAY ST - the house of John Wood the Younger, architect of the Royal Crescent, and son of John Wood the elder, has a turret as it's cornerpiece.

24 WALK AROUND Queen Square, then return to Royal Victoria Park along Royal Avenue. The finish approaches!

Wm WORDSWORTH *poet* 1770-1850, lived in Queen Sq.

HAPPY FAMILIES! Pause awhile and ponder the obelisk in the centre of Queen Square *(left)*, which was erected in 1738 in honour of Prince Frederick *(below)*, at the request of Beau Nash. Frederick, eldest son and heir to George II, was Prince of Wales, but keen historians will already know that he died 9 years before his father, so never became King.

Alas, not everybody liked Prince Frederick; in fact he was positively loathed by his parents! His mother, Queen Caroline, from whom this square takes it's name, called him " the greatest ass and the greatest liar and the greatest canaille and the greatest beast in the whole world, and I heartilly wish he was out of it"! And that was his mum!!

The obelisk was renovated in 1978 to mark both its 250th anniversary, and the Silver Jubillee.

THE NORTH FACADE OF QUEEN SQUARE – was described by R.A.L.Smith as "the true consummation of English Palladian architecture"

THE INSPIRATION FOR A SQUARE ~ Queen Square – named after Queen Caroline – was the very birthplace of the Georgian terrace for which Bath has become so famous. Its architect and driving force was John Wood the Elder, who had been introduced to Bath by the Duke of Chandos. John had been inspired by the Italian architect Andrea Palladio, from which he devised a grand plan to completely rebuild Bath in Italianate style. Not surprisingly, he failed to gain the support of the Corporation *(!)*, but, not disheartened, he decided to implement his plan piecemeal; the first part of which was to be Queen Square.

FIRST he leased the grazing land from the local surgeon Mr Gay *(hence Gay St)*, then designed the square and sub let the sites to individual builders, on condition they erected houses to his exterior design. Building began in December 1728, and was complete by 1735. The resultant square – a masterpiece of contemporary architecture – is roughly 100 metres square with its showpiece on the north side *(see above)*. It attracted such luminary residents as William Wilberforce, William Wordsworth, and Jane Austen. John Wood himself took up residence at number 9, and died there in 1754.

PICTURE POSTCARD VIEW: The resplendent Royal Crescent as seen from Royal Avenue

RETURNING HOME: friends walking through Royal Victoria Park after "Discovering Bath"